TEACHING STUDENTS
WITH
MENTAL
RETARDATION

A PRACTICAL APPROACH TO SPECIAL EDUCATION FOR EVERY TEACHER

The Fundamentals of Special Education
A Practical Guide for Every Teacher

The Legal Foundations of Special Education
A Practical Guide for Every Teacher

Effective Assessment for Students With Special Needs
A Practical Guide for Every Teacher

Effective Instruction for Students With Special Needs
A Practical Guide for Every Teacher

*Working With Families and Community Agencies to
  Support Students With Special Needs*
A Practical Guide for Every Teacher

Public Policy, School Reform, and Special Education
A Practical Guide for Every Teacher

Teaching Students With Sensory Disabilities
A Practical Guide for Every Teacher

Teaching Students With Medical, Physical, and Multiple Disabilities
A Practical Guide for Every Teacher

Teaching Students With Learning Disabilities
A Practical Guide for Every Teacher

Teaching Students With Communication Disorders
A Practical Guide for Every Teacher

Teaching Students With Emotional Disturbance
A Practical Guide for Every Teacher

Teaching Students With Mental Retardation
A Practical Guide for Every Teacher

Teaching Students With Gifts and Talents
A Practical Guide for Every Teacher

TEACHING STUDENTS
WITH
MENTAL
RETARDATION

A Practical Guide for Every Teacher

BOB ALGOZZINE
JIM YSSELDYKE

CORWIN PRESS
A SAGE Publications Company
Thousand Oaks, California

For information:

Corwin Press
A Sage Publications Company
2455 Teller Road
Thousand Oaks, California 91320
www.corwinpress.com

Sage Publications Ltd.
1 Oliver's Yard
55 City Road
London EC1Y 1SP
United Kingdom

Sage Publications India Pvt. Ltd.
B-42, Panchsheel Enclave
Post Box 4109
New Delhi 110 017 India

Printed in the United States of America

Library of Congress Cataloging-in-Publication Data

Algozzine, Robert.
Teaching students with mental retardation : a practical guide for every teacher / Bob Algozzine and James E. Ysseldyke.
    p. cm.
Includes bibliographical references and index.
ISBN 1-4129-3952-6 (cloth) — ISBN 1-4129-3905-4 (pbk.)
   1. Children with mental disabilities—Education—United States.
I. Ysseldyke, James E. II. Title.
LC4631.A72 2006
371.92'8—dc22

                    2006001777

This book is printed on acid-free paper.

06   07   08   09   10   9   8   7   6   5   4   3   2   1

Acquisitions Editor:	Kylee M. Liegl
Editorial Assistant:	Nadia Kashper
Production Editor:	Denise Santoyo
Copy Editor:	Karen E. Taylor
Typesetter:	C&M Digitals (P) Ltd.
Indexer:	Kathy Paparchontis
Cover Designer:	Michael Dubowe

6/12/06 v. 12 of 13

Contents

About
A Practical Approach to Special Education for Every Teacher

S *pecial education* means specially designed instruction for students with unique learning needs. Students receive special education for many reasons. Students with disabilities such as mental retardation, hearing impairments (including deafness), speech or language impairments, visual impairments (including blindness), emotional disturbance, orthopedic impairments, autism, traumatic brain injury, other health impairments, or specific learning disabilities are entitled to special education services. Students who are gifted and talented also receive special education. Special education services are delivered in many settings, including regular classes, resource rooms, and separate classes. The 13 books of this collection will help you teach students with disabilities and those with gifts and talents. Each book focuses on a specific area of special education and can be used individually or in conjunction with all or some of the other books. Six of the books provide the background and content knowledge you need in order to work effectively with all students with unique learning needs:

Book 1: The Fundamentals of Special Education

Book 2: The Legal Foundations of Special Education

Book 3: Effective Assessment for Students With Special Needs

Book 4: Effective Instruction for Students With Special Needs

Book 5: Working With Families and Community Agencies to Support Students With Special Needs

Book 6: Public Policy, School Reform, and Special Education

Seven of the books focus on teaching specific groups of students who receive special education:

Book 7:   Teaching Students With Sensory Disabilities

Book 8:   Teaching Students With Medical, Physical, and Multiple Disabilities

Book 9:   Teaching Students With Learning Disabilities

Book 10: Teaching Students With Communication Disorders

Book 11: Teaching Students With Emotional Disturbance

Book 12: Teaching Students With Mental Retardation

Book 13: Teaching Students With Gifts and Talents

All of the books in *A Practical Approach to Special Education for Every Teacher* will help you to make a difference in the lives of all students, especially those with unique learning needs.

ACKNOWLEDGMENTS

The approach we take in *A Practical Approach to Special Education for Every Teacher* is an effort to change how professionals learn about special education. The 13 separate books are a result of prodding from our students and from professionals in the field to provide a set of materials that "cut to the chase" in teaching them about students with disabilities and about building the capacity of systems to meet those students' needs. Teachers told us that in their classes they always confront students with special learning needs and students their school district has assigned a label to (e.g., students with learning disabilities). Our students and the professionals we worked with wanted a very practical set of texts that gave them the necessary **information** *about* **the students** (e.g., federal definitions, student characteristics) and specific **information on** *what to do about* **the students** (assessment and teaching strategies, approaches that work). They also wanted the opportunity to purchase parts of textbooks, rather than entire texts, to learn what they needed.

The production of this collection would not have been possible without the support and assistance of many colleagues. Professionals associated with Corwin Press—Faye Zucker, Kylee Liegl, Robb Clouse—helped us work through the idea of introducing special education differently, and their support in helping us do it is deeply appreciated.

Faye Ysseldyke and Kate Algozzine, our children, and our grandchildren also deserve recognition. They have made the problems associated with the project very easy to diminish, deal with, or dismiss. Every day in every way, they enrich our lives and make us better. We are grateful for them.

About the Authors

Bob Algozzine, PhD, is Professor in the Department of Educational Leadership at the University of North Carolina at Charlotte and project codirector of the U.S. Department of Education–supported Behavior and Reading Improvement Center. With 25 years of research experience and extensive firsthand knowledge of teaching students classified as seriously emotionally disturbed (and other equally useless terms), Algozzine is a uniquely qualified staff developer, conference speaker, and teacher of behavior management and effective teaching courses.

As an active partner and collaborator with professionals in the Charlotte-Mecklenburg schools in North Carolina and as an editor of several journals focused on special education, Algozzine keeps his finger on the pulse of current special education practice. He has written more than 250 manuscripts on special education topics, authoring many popular books and textbooks on how to manage emotional and social behavior problems. Through *A Practical Approach to Special Education for Every Teacher,* Algozzine hopes to continue to help improve the lives of students with special needs—and the professionals who teach them.

Jim Ysseldyke, PhD, is Birkmaier Professor in the Department of Educational Psychology, director of the School Psychology Program, and director of the Center for Reading Research at the University of Minnesota. Widely requested as a staff developer and conference speaker, he brings more than 30 years of research and teaching experience to educational professionals around the globe.

As the former director of the federally funded National Center on Educational Outcomes, Ysseldyke conducted research and provided technical support that helped to boost the academic performance of students with disabilities and improve school assessment techniques nationally. Today he continues to work to improve the education of students with disabilities.

The author of more than 300 publications on special education and school psychology, Ysseldyke is best known for his textbooks on assessment, effective instruction, issues in special education, and other cutting-edge areas of education and school psychology. With *A Practical Approach to Special Education for Every Teacher*, he seeks to equip educators with practical knowledge and methods that will help them to better engage students in exploring—and meeting—all their potentials.

Self-Assessment 1

B efore you begin this book, check your knowledge of the content being covered. Choose the best answer for each of the following questions.

1. Individuals with mental retardation

   a. do not need to master academic skills

   b. need special assistance to learn what many of their peers learn incidentally

   c. do not have the intelligence to read or do mathematics

   d. represent the largest group of individuals with disabilities receiving special education

2. Even though many states use a variety of terminology to label students who have below average intelligence scores, most of the students

   a. will not be able to live independently

   b. will probably not be able to get a job

   c. have average to low intelligence with average adaptive functioning levels

   d. have significantly subaverage intellectual and adaptive functioning skills

3. There are reasons other than mental retardation that might cause a person to achieve a below average score on an intelligence test, including

   a. civic differences

   b. economic differences

    c. climate differences

    d. cultural differences

4. The addition of _____ to the definition of mental retardation began to improve the problem of overrepresentation of minority students in special education classes.

    a. the adaptive behavior qualifier

    b. the intelligence quotient

    c. current level of functioning

    d. variation in student behavior

5. The definition of mental retardation states that the disability must be diagnosed before the age of

    a. 3

    b. 5

    c. 18

    d. 21

6. According to the definition of mental retardation, how many adaptive skill areas must be limited?

    a. one

    b. more than one

    c. two

    d. more than two

7. Students diagnosed with mental retardation must have an intelligence test score of _____ or below on one or more individually administered general intelligence tests.

    a. 50–55

    b. 60–65

c. 70–75

d. 80–85

8. A student fits the definition of mental retardation if

   a. social problems are prominent

   b. adaptive functioning skills are adequate

   c. adaptive functioning skills are intact

   d. measured intelligence is significantly subaverage

9. The effectiveness with which an individual meets the standards of personal independence and social responsibility expected of his or her age and cultural group is defined as

   a. adaptive behavior

   b. social behavior

   c. peer tolerance behavior

   d. responsible, age-appropriate behavior

10. Adaptive behavior scales may include all of the following except

   a. self-care skills

   b. academic skills

   c. social skills

   d. home living skills

REFLECTION

After you answer the multiple-choice questions, think about how you would answer the following questions:

- What factors might affect the academic success of individuals with mental retardation?
- What are some causes for mental retardation?
- What do effective teachers do to provide support for students with mental retardation?

Introduction to Teaching Students With Mental Retardation

Cecily is a high school freshman who had never taken classes with her peers before eighth grade. The eighth-grade experience was not an easy one. "Inappropriate questions," "frustrated," "no friends," and "always late for class" were words her teachers used to describe the first few weeks of the past school year.

Until last year, Cecily had always been in special education classes. When her parents proposed enrollment in classes with her neighbors and peers without disabilities, school officials were skeptical. The principal noted that there were no special classes in her school and no support system for Cecily. She worried that the transition from middle to high school would be difficult. Nevertheless, the school agreed to give it a try. Now, after a year, the experience is being called a "triumphant success." What happened?

Student volunteers and supportive teachers transformed Cecily's school experiences. Cecily's teachers adapted their lessons and tests for her, and peer "buddies" provided assistance in every class. They helped her focus on what was expected in her assignments, held her to high expectations, and provided feedback on how she was doing. For the first time, Cecily tackled multiplication, division, word problems, and fractions. She gave a presentation in history class and read *The Odyssey*, *To Kill a Mockingbird*, and *Romeo and Juliet* in English class. Why didn't Cecily make this kind of progress before? Her father thinks it's simply because nobody challenged her to do it.

Mental retardation is a disability characterized by significant limitations, both in intellectual functioning and in adaptive behavior as expressed in conceptual, social, and practical adaptive skills (American Association on Mental Retardation, 2002b). Mental retardation is not something you are, like tall or short. Nor is it something you have, like blond hair or long arms. It is not a medical, physical, or health disorder. Mental retardation is a way of functioning that begins in childhood and is characterized by limits in both intelligence and adaptive skills. Mental retardation is reflected in the match between a person's strengths and weaknesses and the structure and expectations of his or her environment.

People with mental retardation need special assistance to learn the tasks that many of their peers learn incidentally. The learning problems caused by mental retardation can create obstacles in many areas of life, and these problems are often aggravated by prejudice and discrimination. With support from families, friends, teachers, neighbors, and peers, students with mental retardation, like Cecily, can be successful in school and in the rest of their lives.

In most school districts across the country, students with mental retardation are being taught in schools and classrooms alongside their neighbors and peers without disabilities. And, that's the way it should be.

Bringing Learning to Life: Using the IEP to Help Cecily Meet Her Educational Goals

An **individualized education program (IEP)** is a specially designed plan that documents current levels of performance; goals, objectives, and services for improving that performance; and dates on which services will be provided, who will provide them, and how they will be monitored to ensure success. Cecily's teachers refer to her long- and short-term objectives in her IEP in order to provide the assistance she needs to succeed—not just in school, but later in life as well. Cecily's IEP addresses the following areas:

Activities for Daily Living Success

Life away from home

Family and personal money management

Childcare and family living

Personal hygiene

Personal independence (food, clothing, shelter)

Personal recreation and leisure

Community living and responsibility

Activities for Personal-Social Success

Self-awareness, self-confidence, social responsibility

Social relations and personal independence

Communication and problem-solving skills

Activities for Occupational Success

Job possibilities

Job requirements

Work habits

Employment skills

While achievement of these goals is important for all students, students with mental retardation often need more assistance than their peers. Career education competencies are considered especially crucial for success in adulthood, so Cecily's teachers make sure to include activities for occupational success in the school day.

1

What Is Mental Retardation?

DEFINITION

The term **mental retardation** is used when mental functioning and deficits in such skills as communicating, taking care of oneself, and functioning socially cause a child to learn and develop more slowly than peers. Children with mental retardation may take longer to learn to speak, walk, and take care of personal needs (such as dressing or eating). In terms of schoolwork, they are able to learn, but they may take longer to master specific skills. Most people with mental retardation learn to do many, many things. It just takes them more time and effort than others.

In the United States, the Individuals With Disabilities Education Act (IDEA), signed into law in 1990, guides schools in providing early intervention, special education, and related services to students with disabilities, including those with mental retardation. It defines **mental retardation** as

> . . . significantly subaverage general intellectual functioning, existing concurrently with deficits in adaptive behavior and manifested during the developmental period, that adversely affects a child's educational performance. (Individuals With Disabilities Education Act, 1990)

9

To diagnose mental retardation, professionals look at both the child's mental abilities and his or her adaptive skills, as IDEA requires. More than 90 percent of all students with mental retardation have **mild mental retardation** (see *Figure 1.1*). This group is sometimes referred to as "educable mentally retarded." Most of the states that offer special education services for students with mild mental retardation use IQs (intelligence quotients) between 50 and 70 as a partial basis for determining eligibility. (These scores are more than two standard deviations below the mean.)

States use IQs of between 35–40 and 50–55 to determine eligibility for services for **moderate retardation** (see *Table 1.1*). This group of students, sometimes referred to as "trainable mentally retarded," represents about 5 percent of all students with mental retardation.

Students with **moderate, severe, or profound retardation** need ongoing assistance in most areas of practical living skills and are generally more dependent on others for care. This is the smallest group of students with mental retardation (less than 2 percent).

Figure 1.1   Relations Between Mild, Moderate, Severe, and Profound Retardation

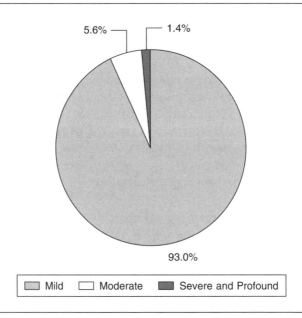

Table 1.1 Levels of Retardation

Severity	IQ Range
Mild	50-55 to 70-75
Moderate	35-40 to 50-55
Severe	20-25 to 35-40
Profound	Below 20-25

PREVALENCE

As many as 3 out of every 100 people in the United States have mental retardation (American Association on Mental Retardation, 2002b), and rates in Canada are similar to those in the United States. Almost 613,000 children aged 6–21 have some level of mental retardation and need special education (U.S. Department of Education, 2002). In fact, 1 out of every 10 children receives special education because of some form of mental retardation.

2

What Causes Mental Retardation?

Mental retardation is neither a disease nor a physical illness, so there is no medical treatment for it. You cannot "catch" it from someone. Scientists have found many causes of mental retardation. The most common are genetic conditions, problems during pregnancy, problems at birth, and general health problems.

GENETIC CONDITIONS

Mental retardation may be caused by abnormal genes inherited from parents, errors when genes combine, or other gene-related problems. Examples of genetic conditions are Down's syndrome, Klinefelter's syndrome, and phenylketonuria (PKU).

Nearly all of the genetic syndromes that result in mental retardation also cause outward physical traits. Those who have **Down's syndrome**, a condition in which the 21st set of chromosomes is a triplet rather than a pair, usually have a rounder face and shorter limbs than others their age. They also have decreased muscle tone (hypotonia), hyperflexibility of joints, smaller oral cavities (causing tongue protrusion), and short, broad hands with a single palmar crease; they sometimes suffer heart, eye, respiratory, or ear problems.

Klinefelter's syndrome is a combination of physical abnormalities that typically result from aberrations in the sex chromosomes—pair 23 (the male has an extra X chromosome). These abnormalities become apparent only at and after puberty, and can include gynecomastia (development of female secondary sex characteristics), small testes, poor hair growth, and mental retardation.

Unlike Down's syndrome and Klinefelter syndrome, phenylketonuria (PKU) does not necessarily cause outward physical traits. **Phenylketonuria (PKU)** is an inherited genetic metabolic disorder in which the enzyme required to digest phenylalanine (PHE), a part of protein, is missing. If untreated, this deficiency leads to high levels of PHE in the blood, which can affect brain development and learning.

Understanding Down's Syndrome

Down's syndrome is a common type of mental retardation; it accounts for about 10 percent of all instances of moderate and severe retardation. Down's syndrome is a chromosomal abnormality. The nucleus of each human cell contains 23 pairs of chromosomes. In the most common type of Down's syndrome, trisomy 21, the twenty-first pair has three rather than two chromosomes.

Some physical characteristics, such as small stature, short and broad hands, and epicanthic folds (an extra flap of skin over the innermost corners of the eyes), are usually present in people with Down's syndrome. Identification in infancy is common. The severity of retardation evident with Down's syndrome is usually related to the age at which it is detected. Early identification and intervention result in less severe effects. Today, many students with Down's syndrome are being educated in general education classrooms with their neighbors and peers.

Problems During Pregnancy and Birth

Mental retardation can result when the fetus does not develop properly. For example, there may be a problem with the way the cells divide as the embryo or fetus grows. Drinking alcohol or contracting rubella (German measles) during pregnancy may also cause mental retardation of the baby. During labor and birth, a baby may become mentally retarded if it doesn't receive adequate oxygen to the brain.

Health Problems

Diseases like whooping cough, measles, and meningitis can cause mental retardation. Mental retardation can also be caused by extreme malnutrition, inadequate medical care, or by exposure to poisons like lead and mercury.

3

How Is Mental Retardation Diagnosed?

Mental retardation is diagnosed by looking at two areas: intellectual functioning and adaptive behavior. **Intellectual functioning** is the person's ability to learn, think, solve problems, and make sense of the world. Intellectual functioning is commonly measured by administering an IQ test. The average score on an IQ test is 100. People scoring below 70–75 are thought to have mental retardation.

The other area that professionals consider when mental retardation is suspected is adaptive behavior. **Adaptive behavior**, sometimes called adaptive functioning, is a person's ability to learn and apply life skills in ways that enable him or her to live independently. To measure adaptive behavior, professionals look at what a person can do in comparison to others of the same age. They observe adaptive behaviors in three areas:

1. Daily living skills (e.g., getting dressed, going to the bathroom, and feeding one's self)

2. Communication skills (e.g., understanding what is said and being able to answer)

3. Social skills (e.g., positive interactions with peers, family members, adults, and others)

Providing services to those with mental retardation has led to a new understanding of its diagnosis. After the initial diagnosis of mental retardation is made, professionals consider the person's strengths and weaknesses. They also look at how much support or help the person needs to get along at home, in school, and in the community. This approach provides a more realistic picture of an individual's needs. It also recognizes that the "picture" changes. As an individual grows and learns, his or her ability to get along in the world grows as well. Schools use a number of different terms with regard to mental retardation, including "educationally retarded," "educational handicap," "mental handicap," "severe handicap," and "significantly limited intellectual capability." Some states in the U.S. deliver services to students with mental retardation on a **noncategorical** basis (i.e., without formally labeling them), although this is fairly uncommon.

In addition to the definitions for mental retardation previously noted, the definition provided by the American Association on Mental Retardation (AAMR, 2002a) is helpful for diagnosis:

> Mental retardation is a disability characterized by significant limitations both in intellectual functioning and in adaptive behavior as expressed in conceptual, social, and practical adaptive skills. This disability originates before age 18. (¶ 5)

The conceptual framework for this definition rests on several assumptions (American Association on Mental Retardation, 2002b):

> Limitations in functioning must be considered within the context of environments that are typical of the individual's peers and culture.

> Appropriate assessment considers cultural and linguistic diversity as well as differences in communication and sensory, motor, and behavior factors.

> For most people, limitations coexist with strengths.

> A primary reason for identifying limitations is to develop a profile of needed supports.

> With appropriate personalized supports over a sustained period, the life functioning of the person with mental retardation generally will improve.

When using the AAMR definition for identification, classification, and intervention planning, educators must

View limitations in present functioning within the context of the individual's peers and culture;

Take into account the individual's cultural and linguistic differences as well as communication, sensory, motor, and behavior skills;

Describe limitations so that individualized supports can be developed; and

Provide appropriate supports to improve the functioning of a person with mental retardation.

Educators typically rely on test scores and other information as evidence of significant limitations in intellectual functioning and adaptive behavior. For example, over the years, an IQ of 70–75 or below has been used as one indication of mental retardation. However, *limitations in adaptive behavior must occur at the same time as limitations in intellectual functioning.* Limited intellectual functioning alone is insufficient for a diagnosis of mental retardation. Further, more than one area of functioning (e.g., conceptual, social, and practical adaptive skills) must be limited. Mental retardation is viewed as a disorder of childhood, that is, it originates before age 18, the life period of greatest expected development.

Significance of Adaptive
Behavior in Diagnosis

There was a time when mental retardation was simply defined as significantly below average intelligence. Because low scores on intelligence tests could result for reasons other than mental retardation (e.g., cultural differences, language differences), special classes were overpopulated with inappropriate groups (e.g., culturally disadvantaged students). Needless to say, no one was happy—not parents, not educators, and not students. The addition of the adaptive behavior "qualifier" stopped the crowding of classes with students who would be best served in other ways.

Figures 3.1a and *3.1b* show that before the adaptive behavior qualifier, students with significantly subaverage intelligence were classified with retardation, regardless of their behavioral functioning. Now, students fit the definition of mental retardation only if measured intelligence is significantly subaverage *and* adaptive behavior deficits are present.

Whenever professionals try to define adaptive behavior, they come up against the same variables that make defining normal behavior a difficult process. The decision about the extent to which a person's behavior is adaptive is a subjective one; it depends largely on the standards of the individuals making the judgment and the environment to which the student is expected to adapt. There is no definition of adaptive behavior in the federal rules, but, generally, the term refers to the ways in which an individual functions in his or her social environment. The AAMR (formerly

Figures 3.1a and 3.1b   Including "Adaptive Behavior" in the Definition of Mental Retardation Changed Who Received Services.

Adaptive Behavior Deficits			
	Yes	Mental Retardation	Not Mental Retardation
	No	Mental Retardation	Not Mental Retardation

Figure 3.1a   Before Adaptive Behavior Was Added to the Definition

Adaptive Behavior Deficits			
	Yes	Mental Retardation	Not Mental Retardation
	No	Not Mental Retardation	Not Mental Retardation

Figure 3.1b   After Adaptive Behavior Was Added to the Definition

the American Association on Mental Deficiency) defined **adaptive behavior** as

> The effectiveness or degree with which the individual meets the standards of personal independence and social responsibility expected of his/her age and cultural group. (Grossman, 1983, p. 1)

Within the context of the AAMR definition of mental retardation, **adaptive behavior** is a collection of conceptual, social, and practical skills that enables a person to function in everyday life. The AAMR considers the ten adaptive skill areas in *Table 3.1* important for people with and without disabilities. Limitations in two or more of these adaptive skill areas are required for a diagnosis of mental retardation. Clinical judgments, environmental expectations, and potential support systems are considered when adaptive behavior is evaluated.

Table 3.1   Adaptive Skill Areas Evaluated in Diagnosing Mental Retardation

Skill Area	Description
Communication	• Understanding information provided through speech • Understanding information provided through written words, symbols, sign language, facial expressions, body movements, or other gestures • Providing information using speech, written words, symbols, sign language, facial expressions, body movements, or other gestures
Community Living	• Interacting with neighbors and community members • Participating in recreation and leisure activities • Shopping

(Continued)

Table 3.1 (Continued)

Skill Area	Description
	• Using public buildings, settings, and other facilities • Using public and private transportation systems • Visiting friends and family
Employment	• Accessing and obtaining help and assistance at work • Changing work assignments • Completing work-related tasks • Interacting with supervisors • Interacting with co-workers • Learning and using work-related behaviors
Functional Academics	Practical learning related to • Reading • Writing • Mathematics • Science • Geography • Social Studies
Health and Safety	• Accessing emergency services and assistance • Avoiding health and safety hazards • Communicating with health care providers • Maintaining a healthy diet • Maintaining mental health/emotional well-being • Maintaining physical health • Obtaining medical assistance and services • Taking medication
Home Living	• Bathing • Cleaning and housekeeping • Dressing

Skill Area	Description
	• Laundering and taking care of clothes • Operating small appliances and technology • Participating in leisure activities at home • Preparing and eating food alone or with others • Taking care of grooming and personal hygiene • Toileting
Leisure	• Beginning, extending, and ending activities with others • Playing appropriately with others • Taking turns
Self-Care and Advocacy	• Banking, cashing checks, and using money • Belonging to and participating in support group • Defending self and others • Exercising legal rights and responsibilities • Managing money and other finances • Obtaining legal services • Protecting self from exploitation
Social Skills	• Communicating with others about personal needs • Engaging in positive, intimate relationships • Making appropriate sexual decisions • Making and keeping friends • Offering assistance and assisting others • Participating in recreation and leisure activities • Socializing within the family

Window on Practice: Adaptive Behavior Scales

There are dozens of **adaptive behavior scales**. They typically contain items related to self-care, communication, academic and social skills, home living, community use, health, safety, and work. The items usually require parents, teachers, or others familiar with the student's current functioning to respond to questions such as these:

1. Some children are afraid of lots of things. How about _____ ? (name of child)

    a. is afraid of many things

    b. is afraid of a few things

    c. is not afraid of much

2. How does _____ (name of child) get along with peers at school?

    a. not very well

    b. fairly well

    c. very well

People familiar with an individual's response to the daily demands of home, school, work, and community environments are best qualified to evaluate adaptive behavior.

Because expectations vary by age group, so do the criteria used to identify deficits in adaptive behavior at specific ages. Grossman (1983) linked the criteria for identifying adaptive behavior to developmental stages.

During infancy and early childhood, deficits appear in

- Development of sensorimotor skills
- Communication skills (including speech and language)

- Self-help skills
- Socialization (ability to interact with others)

During childhood and early adolescence, deficits appear in all the areas listed above and/or in the

- Application of basic academic skills in daily life activities
- Application of appropriate reasoning and judgment in mastery of the environment
- Application of social skills to participation in group activities and interpersonal relationships

During late adolescence and adult life, deficits appear in all the areas listed above and/or in

- Vocational and social responsibilities and performance

The adaptive-behavior criterion is critical for identifying students with mental retardation. People who function adequately outside school are not considered to have mental retardation, even if they perform poorly on intelligence tests.

4

What Characteristics Are Associated With Mental Retardation?

Regardless of the severity of their mental retardation, students today are receiving substantial portions of their instruction alongside their peers who do not have disabilities.

About 90 percent of people with mental retardation are only slightly below average in learning new information and skills. As young children, their limitations are not always obvious. They may not be diagnosed as having mental retardation until they begin school. As they become adults, they are able to live independently. Their neighbors and coworkers may not even be aware of their mental retardation.

The remaining 10 percent of people with mental retardation score below 50 on IQ tests. They have more difficulty getting along in school, at home, and in the community. The more severe the retardation, the more intensive the support needed. Every individual with mental retardation is able to learn, develop, and grow, no matter how severe his or her condition. They can live rich, satisfying lives.

Early researchers focused many of their efforts on describing the characteristics of students with mental retardation. Primary indications include rates of learning that are slower than those of peers and evidence of delays in most areas of development. For example, a seven-year-old child with mental retardation may be just beginning to demonstrate skills (e.g., naming colors, counting numbers, writing the alphabet) that same-age peers demonstrated several years earlier. Similarly, whereas students with learning disabilities or communication disorders often display discrepancies in performance in selected areas, students with mental retardation fail to meet expectations in several areas—cognitive, academic, physical, behavioral, and communication.

Mental retardation can also be a secondary condition, coexisting with another exceptionality. There is considerable overlap between the kinds of characteristics said to be exhibited by students with mental retardation and those attributed to students with learning disabilities or behavior disorders. For example, students with mental retardation and those with learning disabilities may demonstrate attentional, memory, motor, and information-processing disorders. Students with mental retardation and those with behavior disorders may be anxious, have temper tantrums, be overly aggressive, disruptive, dependent, and impulsive. It is almost impossible, then, to identify characteristics that are universal or specific to students with mental retardation. The representative characteristics and potential problems of students with mental retardation are presented in *Table 4.1*. Teaching students with mental retardation means addressing specific challenges and their associated problems:

Cognitive challenges

Academic challenges

Physical challenges

Behavioral challenges

Communication challenges

Table 4.1   Representative Characteristics and Concomitant
Problems of Mental Retardation

Area	Characteristics	Potential Problems
Cognitive	Limited memory Limited general knowledge and information Concrete rather than abstract thinking Slower learning rate	Inattention Inefficient learning style Difficulty communicating Prone to failure Standard teaching practices ineffective
Academic	Difficulty learning most academic content Limited performance in most content areas Limited problem-solving ability Limited content mastery	Limited attention, organizational skills, questioning behaviors, direction following, monitoring of time, and other school coping skills
Physical	Some discrepancies between physical and mental abilities	Performance often less than expected, based on physical appearance
Behavioral	Limited social and personal competence Limited coping skills Limited personal life skills and competence	Tardiness, complaints of illness, classroom disruptiveness, social isolation, inappropriate activity
Communication	Lower levels of language development, limited listening and speaking vocabularies	Difficulty following directions, making requests, interacting, or communicating

COGNITIVE

By definition, students with mental retardation show delayed cognitive functioning. A low score or set of scores on one or more intelligence tests is a diagnostic criterion of the condition and its severity (see *Table 1.1*). In addition to not learning as effectively or efficiently as their peers, students with mental retardation are often slow to generalize and conceptualize and may have weak comprehension skills. They may demonstrate limited short-term memory and have difficulty in discrimination, sequencing, and identifying analogies. They may also be less able than their peers to grasp abstract concepts. These cognitive deficits are considered the primary cause of their academic difficulties.

ACADEMIC

Students with mental retardation perform poorly in most academic areas, but at a level in line with what is expected based on their scores on intelligence tests. This consistency between expectation and performance is one distinction between mental retardation and learning disabilities. (Students with learning disabilities show a discrepancy in their scores on intelligence tests [expectation] and their scores on achievement tests [performance].) Still another distinction is in the breadth of deficient performance. Students with mental retardation typically perform poorly in the majority of academic subject areas; students with learning disabilities often demonstrate specific areas of academic difficulty.

PHYSICAL

Although some students with mental retardation appear physically different from others, most students with mental retardation do not look different from their peers. However, some of their physical abilities (e.g., gross and fine motor coordination, mobility) may be different.

Most students with severe mental retardation have limited physical mobility. Many cannot walk, and some cannot stand or sit up without support. They are slow to perform physical movements (e.g., rolling over, grasping toys and objects, raising the head) that are easy for peers without mental retardation.

BEHAVIORAL

Researchers have not been able to identify social and emotional characteristics that are specific to students with mental retardation, probably because each student is unique and interindividual variation is considerable, both in level of retardation and in the kinds of characteristics displayed. By definition, individuals with mental retardation exhibit socially inappropriate behaviors; often they are both socially and emotionally immature. Inappropriate behaviors, antisocial behaviors, and odd mannerisms can lead others to reject those with mental retardation. Some people with severe or profound retardation have difficulty with independent living skills, such as dressing, eating, exercising, bowel and bladder control, and maintaining personal hygiene. Often, they must be cared for throughout their lives. People with severe retardation may also require special instruction involving adaptive devices (e.g., specially designed eating utensils) or adapted learning sequences (e.g., task-analyzed hierarchies) to learn basic skills.

COMMUNICATION

Conceptual development and language are closely related. Individuals who show delayed cognitive functioning typically show delayed development of language and communication skills.

Students with mental retardation may have difficulty expressing themselves well enough to be understood. This limitation is especially true of those with severe or profound retardation. Almost all students with severe mental retardation are limited in their ability to express themselves or understand others. Many do not talk or use gestures to communicate; and they may not respond to communication from others. Those with mild retardation sometimes demonstrate delayed comprehension as well as receptive and expressive language problems.

In your classroom, if a student is having difficulty in the following areas, you may refer him or her to your school psychologist, a child-study team, or another professional for assessment:

- Sitting up, crawling, and walking
- Learning to talk or speaking in general
- Remembering things
- Understanding how to pay for things
- Understanding social rules
- Seeing the consequences of his or her actions
- Solving problems
- Thinking logically

5

How Should Teachers Teach Students With Mental Retardation?

A child with mental retardation can do well in school but is likely to need individualized help. Fortunately, in the United States, each state is responsible for meeting the educational needs of children with disabilities.

For children up to age 3, services are provided through an early intervention system. Staff members work with the child's family to develop what is known as an **individualized family services plan**, or IFSP. The IFSP describes the child's unique needs and the services that will address those needs. It emphasizes the unique needs of the family and outlines how family members can help the child. Early intervention services are provided at no cost if a family qualifies.

For eligible school-aged children (including preschoolers), special education and related services are available through the school system. School staff works with the student's family to develop an **individualized education program**, or IEP. An IEP is similar to an IFSP. It describes the student's unique needs and the services designed to meet those needs. Special education and related services are provided at no cost to the family.

The adaptive-behavior criterion that is now part of the definition of mental retardation is central to planning interventions for students. Instruction is directed at areas crucial to successful adaptation in school, home, and community, not just in typical academic areas (e.g., reading, writing, arithmetic).

Many students with mental retardation need help with adaptive skills (the skills needed to live, work, and play in the community). Teachers and family members can help the student develop many adaptive skills, including

Communicating with others

Taking care of personal needs (e.g., dressing, bathing, going to the bathroom)

Staying healthy and safe

Home living (e.g., helping to set the table, cleaning the house, cooking dinner)

Using social skills (e.g., manners, knowing the rules of conversation, getting along in a group, playing a game)

Reading, writing, and basic math

Workplace skills

You can help students with mental retardation by making **adaptations** (supports or changes in the classroom). Some common adaptations are offered in *Table 5.1*. In addition, the organizations listed in the Resources section are great for learning specific techniques and strategies that support students who have mental retardation. When you are working with the family of a student who has mental retardation, offer support and suggestions for reinforcing skill use at home. *Table 5.2* provides tips specifically for families.

Students with mental retardation need assistance learning the content and skills that many of their peers learn without special educational activities. Many of the activities that are appropriate for teaching basic academic skills (e.g., reading, writing, and arithmetic) to students with learning disabilities and speech and language problems are appropriate for students with mental retardation.

You can assist students with mental retardation by making what they are learning relevant to real-life experiences (i.e., functional skills) and by adjusting how they approach learning activities (i.e., school adaptive behavior). Effective teachers of students with mental retardation set high expectations for

Table 5.1   Tips for Teachers

Seven Ways to Help Students Overcome Challenges Posed by Mental Retardation

1. Recognize that you can make an enormous difference in the student's life. Find out what the student's strengths and interests are, and emphasize them. Create opportunities for success.

2. If you are not part of the student's individualized education program (IEP) team, ask for a copy of his or her IEP. The student's educational goals will be listed there, as well as the services and classroom adaptations required. Talk to the specialists in your school as necessary. They can help you identify effective methods of teaching the student, recommend adaptations to the curriculum, and offer pointers on how to address the student's IEP goals in your classroom.

3. Be as concrete as possible. Demonstrate what you mean rather than just giving verbal directions. Relate new information verbally, but also show a picture. In addition to showing the picture, provide hands-on materials and opportunities for the student to try things out.

4. Break long, new tasks into short steps and demonstrate the steps. Have the student do the steps, one at a time, providing assistance as necessary.

5. Give the student immediate feedback.

6. Teach daily living skills and social skills, and provide occupational awareness and exploration as appropriate. Involve the student in group activities or clubs.

7. Work together with the student's family and other school personnel to create and implement an educational plan tailored to meet the student's needs. Regularly share information about how the student is progressing at school and at home.

achievement and focus their instruction on functional activities designed to promote success with real-life problems. A summary of general interventions is presented in *Table 5.3.* Specific activities for improving functional skills, school adaptive behavior, and leisure and work skills are discussed in the following section.

Table 5.2   Eight Ways Families Can Help Children Overcome
Challenges Posed by Mental Retardation

1. Learn more about mental retardation. The more you know, the more you can help yourself and your child. Ask school staff to recommend organizations to contact and other resources.

2. Encourage independence. Help your child learn daily care skills, such as dressing, eating, using the bathroom, and grooming.

3. Give your child chores to do. Keep his or her age, attention span, and abilities in mind. Break jobs into smaller steps. For example, for setting the table, first ask your child to get the right number of napkins. Then have your child put one at each place at the table. Do the same with the utensils, one at a time. Tell your child what to do, step by step, until the job is done. Demonstrate how to do the job. Help your child when he or she needs assistance.

4. Give your child frequent feedback. Praise your child when he or she does well. Build your child's abilities.

5. Find out what skills your child is learning at school. Provide opportunities for your child to apply those skills at home. For example, if your child is learning about money in school, the next time you are at the supermarket, help your child count out the money to pay for the groceries. Then help count the change.

6. Find opportunities for your child to participate in social activities, such as scouts, recreation center activities, and sports. Group activities will help your child build social skills and have fun.

7. Talk to other parents whose children have mental retardation. Call the National Information Center for Children and Youth with Disabilities (NICHCY) at (800) 695-0285. Ask how to find a parent group near you.

8. Meet with school staff to develop an educational plan to address your child's individual needs. Keep in touch with your child's teachers, and find out how you can support your child's school learning at home.

Table 5.3   Top Ten Tips for Teachers of Students with Mental Retardation

1. Use varied examples in your instructional presentations. Focus on functional skills.

2. Provide opportunities for students to actively demonstrate understanding before moving to independent practice.

3. Provide more opportunities for practice than may be appropriate or necessary for classmates.

4. Use concrete examples when teaching new skills.

5. Provide supportive and corrective feedback more often than may be necessary for classmates.

6. Modify tests and evaluation measures to compensate for learning problems.

7. Evaluate student performance and progress more frequently than may be appropriate or necessary for classmates.

8. Adapt instruction to the environments where the skills or knowledge will be applied.

9. Break lessons into smaller parts when teaching complex skills.

10. Be prepared to repeat teaching more frequently than necessary for peers.

IMPROVING FUNCTIONAL ACADEMIC SKILLS

Students with mental retardation respond to the same instructional methods as other students, though they may require more time to achieve mastery. Typically, they require special instruction and extra practice to generalize what they have learned to settings other than the classroom. Sometimes, they simply need to be taught how to approach academic tasks; often, they need skill instruction beyond basal readers and traditional worksheets. To be effective, teachers design instructional and practice activities so that they relate to applications in everyday life, including home living and community use.

Task Completion

The following two strategies will help you encourage students with mental retardation to complete assignments:

1. **To reduce task avoidance, use random checks to monitor behavior.** Set an inexpensive kitchen timer to beep at randomly selected amounts of time during independent activities. Reward students who are working when the timer sounds.

2. **To improve task completion, reward processes, not just products.** Completion of most classroom assignments can be broken into three main activities: starting, working, and finishing. For some students with mental retardation, simply getting started is a major accomplishment. Sometimes, providing more frequent rewards (e.g., for starting and working) helps these students complete more work. Also, allowing them to select "where to start" and "how much to do before a break" can be helpful in improving the number of tasks they complete.

Functional Reading

1. **To improve functional reading, create practice worksheets using everyday materials.** Use common signs (e.g., men, women, street names, business names), restaurant menus, selected sections of the newspaper (e.g., advertisements, sports), food labels, favorite foods, names of toys or games, television programs, sports teams, or community helpers (e.g., mayor, sheriff, police) to create practice reading worksheets. Model the sheets on those being used with other reading materials, or make up some of your own. See *Figure 5.1* for an example.

2. **To improve functional reading, have students read the actual materials used in everyday life.** Using a local phone book, have students find numbers for classmates, teachers, friends, relatives, businesses, restaurants, movie theatres, and community agencies (e.g., library, post office).

Figure 5.1   Worksheet to Improve Functional Reading

Put these streets in alphabetical order.

Redcoat Lane	1. *Allendale Lane*
East Boulevard	2. _____
West Boulevard	3. _____
Allendale Lane	4. _____
Sardis Road	5. _____
Brentwood Drive	6. _____
Randolph Road	7. _____
Castle Street	8. _____
Oldtowne Road	9. _____
Walker Place	10. _____

3. **To improve functional reading, place words from functional reading vocabulary into word puzzles.** You can create simple crossword puzzles or word-search puzzles using software such as *Crossword Magic* (Mindscape) or *WordSearch Deluxe* (Nordic Software). Have students prepare their own puzzles and exchange them with other classes in the school.

4. **To improve functional reading, play games.** Once students have learned a list of words, use them in games like Bingo and Concentration (see *Figures 5.2a* and *5.2b*). For Bingo, have students prepare a card using words they are practicing. Select one student to be the "caller," and have others play Bingo using poker chips, paper clips, or other markers to keep track of words as they are called. Have students decide the criterion for winning a game (e.g., straight line vertically, diagonal line, or four

corners). For Concentration, have students put each word on two different index cards. Shuffle the cards and place them face down on a desk. Have students play the Concentration game by turning the cards over two at a time to find matches. Control the difficulty by controlling the number of cards being used. Encourage social interaction by having two or more students play together.

Functional Writing

1. **To improve functional writing, use daily living activities.** Use activities of daily living to practice writing, spelling, and handwriting. Have students keep diaries of school activities, make lists of things to do, list things that were done during the school day, practice taking telephone messages, complete job applications, order products from catalogs, write messages for parents describing upcoming school activities, and write letters to classmates and pen pals in other classrooms, schools, states, and countries.

Figure 5.2a Examples of Bingo

Bingo

Bobby's card

B	I	N	G	O
wait	walk	stop	street	job
help	cost	bill	safe	worker
work	hours	**FREE**	wages	tax
check	bank	taxi	bus	boss
pay	store	food	enter	order

Jimmy's card

B	I	N	G	O
job	worker	tax	boss	order
street	safe	wages	enter	bus
stop	bill	**FREE**	taxi	food
walk	cost	hours	store	bank
wait	help	work	check	pay

Figure 5.2b Example of Concentration

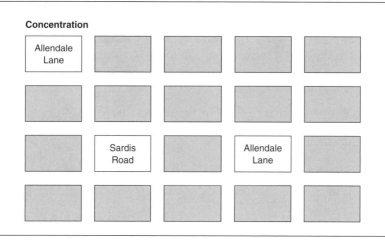

Functional Math

1. **To improve basic math skills, use software.** Have students practice simple math operations (e.g., addition, subtraction, multiplication, and division) with software like *Number Munchers* (MECC). Keep records of performance improvements in accuracy and rate of completion for 10 and 20 problem sets.

2. **To improve functional math skills, have students practice with real-life problems.** Everyday math skills are most commonly used in areas involving time, money, and measurement. Students with mental retardation need to practice these skills more than their peers do. Prepare assignments on making change, keeping track of checking or savings account balances, doing comparison shopping, and keeping track of a weekly budget. Create problems on measurement (e.g., size of objects in the room, outside school, in the home) and time (e.g., telling time, using calendars, keeping schedules) to provide additional functional math practice.

3. **To improve functional math skills, have students practice on classroom field trips.** A field trip is an experience designed to add to ongoing instructional programs. Most of the time, field trips are elaborate, well-planned visits to businesses, museums, or other places away from school.

In-class field trips can serve the same purposes. For example, functional math field trips can provide the experience of searching for specific information in newspapers or magazines in the classroom or at a local business (see *Figure 5.3*). The key is to have a specific set of activities for students to accomplish while on the field trip.

Figure 5.3   In-Class Field Trip Example

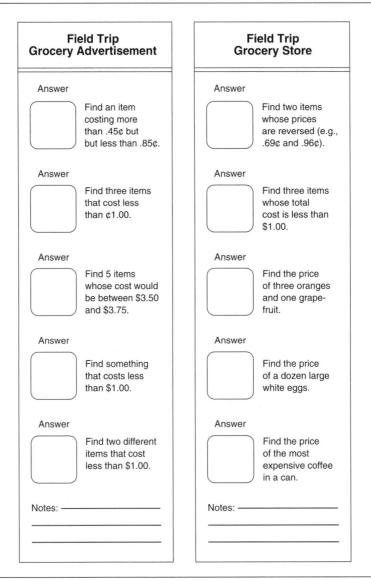

Bringing Learning to Life:
Task Analysis Helped Cecily's Teachers

Cecily's teachers were interested in making what they were teaching in science relevant to her daily life. They decided that first-aid skills were appropriate instructional objectives in areas related to personal hygiene and community living and responsibility. They located articles in professional journals that described procedures for teaching first-aid skills to students with mental retardation (Spooner, Stem, & Test, 1989; Stem & Test, 1989). They used the information in the articles to plan instructional units for Cecily and her classmates.

The teachers identified important first-aid skills: communicating an emergency, applying a plastic bandage, and taking care of minor injuries. Then they used **task analysis** (breaking complex skills into component parts) to establish an appropriate teaching sequence and to decide which skill to teach first (least complex). The teachers then gathered baseline information on the extent to which Cecily was able to respond appropriately to mock situations involving first-aid skills (see the diagram that follows on p. 45).

One teacher demonstrated the correct execution of the skill. She then asked Cecily to demonstrate the skill. During this phase, the teacher provided verbal praise (supportive feedback) for Cecily's correct responses and corrective feedback (verbal redirecting, another example, or physical guidance) for incorrect responses.

When Cecily reached acceptable levels of performance (80 percent accuracy), the teacher had her practice the skill independently and provided supportive and corrective feedback less frequently. When Cecily had completed the instructional sequence, her teacher asked to "prove" that she had learned the first-aid skills by responding to mock situations without her assistance. She compared Cecily's performance before and after intervention to evaluate the effectiveness of the lessons and her instruction (see p. 45).

(continued)

Mock Situation for Communicating an Emergency

For the skill of communicating an emergency, Cecily's teachers used the following mock situation:

You and your friend are at a restaurant eating lunch. Your friend is laughing and talking while eating and begins to choke on a piece of hamburger. He first begins to cough. Then he is unable to cough, breathe, or speak. What do you do?

For the skills of applying a plastic bandage and taking care of minor injuries, the teachers constructed similar mock situations. To evaluate Cecily's responses, they used the following task analyses.

Task Analyses

Communicating an emergency

1. Locate phone.
2. Pick up receiver.
3. Dial 9.
4. Dial 1.
5. Dial 1.
6. Put receiver to your ear.
7. Listen for operator.
8. Give full name.
9. Give full address.
10. Give phone number.
11. Explain emergency.
12. Hang up after operator does.

Applying a plastic bandage

1. Look at injury.
2. Find bandages needed.
3. Select proper size.
4. Find outside tabs of wrapper.
5. Pull down tabs to expose bandage.
6. Find protective covering on bandage.
7. Pull off tabs to expose gauze portion.
8. Do not touch gauze portion.
9. Apply to clean, dry skin.

Taking care of minor injuries

1. Let it bleed a little to wash out the dirt.
2. Wash with soap and water.
3. Dry with a clean cloth.

Evaluating Cecily's Performance

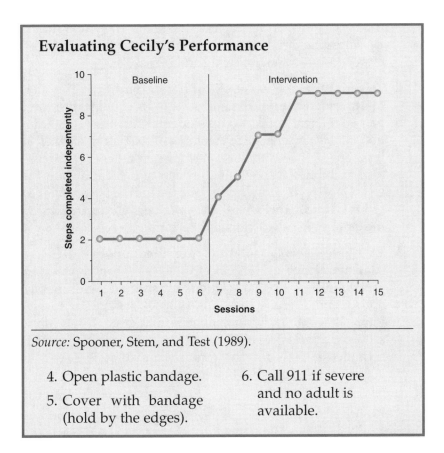

Source: Spooner, Stem, and Test (1989).

4. Open plastic bandage.

5. Cover with bandage (hold by the edges).

6. Call 911 if severe and no adult is available.

IMPROVING SCHOOL ADAPTIVE BEHAVIOR

School adaptive behaviors—including social skills, self-direction, self-care, and health and safety—are intervention targets for students with mental retardation. Improving the social repertoire of any student is not easy, and it is especially difficult for students experiencing adaptive behavior deficits. The following strategies will help you address adaptive behaviors in your classroom.

Social Skills

1. **To improve social skills, create a play.** Create a play in which appropriate social skills are demonstrated in everyday activities (e.g., greeting friends or working on a group

project). Reward the actors for their demonstrations. Be sure the student with mental retardation has an opportunity to see the play and be an actor.

2. **To reduce social isolation, initiate group activities that foster socialization.** Organize a group spelling test, and pair competent spellers with students with mental retardation. Make a rule that each member of the pair must spell at least one word on the test. Encourage students to discuss responsibilities (i.e., who will spell each word) during the test. Once pairs are working successfully, change pairs to groups. Gradually increase the size of the group, increasing the amount of interaction and performance required.

3. **To reduce social isolation, provide opportunities for sharing.** Active participation in classroom activities can greatly improve social relations for students with mental retardation. Identify the skills, hobbies, general or special interests, and individual experiences (e.g., trips, after-school activities) of each of your students. Plan group activities to share this information, and allow students to get to know each other better.

Self-Direction

1. **To improve self-direction and self-management, provide signals for students.** Some students with mental retardation have not learned ways to let others know they need help. Some teachers create a signal system to replace unacceptable alternatives (e.g., blurting out, wild hand waving, not asking). For example, a small NEED HELP sign is a useful way for a student to get a teacher's attention without distracting others.

2. **To improve self-direction and self-management, have students practice and discuss skills.** Select "problem situations," and discuss the best ways to react when faced with them. Have students generate, discuss, and practice as many alternatives as possible.

3. **To improve self-direction and self-management, help students keep track of good behavior.** Place an index card

on the corner of the student's desk for use in keeping track of appropriate behaviors (e.g., completing assignments, asking for help). Periodically check the card to be sure the student is monitoring appropriate behaviors. Have students with mental retardation share their self-reports with classmates and parents as a means of promoting positive self-concepts and pride in independent behavior.

Self-Care

1. **To improve self-care, health, and safety skills, have students practice and discuss appropriate behaviors.** Create mock situations, and have students generate, discuss, and practice appropriate solutions.

Students with mild and moderate mental retardation experience difficulties in many areas of school and life functioning. There are no magic instructional activities that work with all these students all the time, just as not all teaching strategies work always with other students. Whenever necessary, effective teachers modify what they do to accommodate the special learning needs of their students. With this type of instruction, students with mild or moderate mental retardation can learn to overcome many of their problems and can be successful and productive in school and life experiences. A key here is the importance of high expectations: If we think we can, we will find a way. If we think we can't, we will not.

Bringing Learning to Life:
Differential Grading Helped Cecily's Teachers

Cecily's teachers decided to use different systems when assigning in-class, homework, special project, and report card grades. Sometimes they used simplified grades to reflect her performance, such as

(continued)

(continued)

Pass/Needs Improvement/Fail

Acceptable/Unacceptable

At other times, Cecily's teachers assigned one grade for achievement and another for effort. They also used combinations of three traditional grading systems:

1. *Grade level appraisal:* Cecily's current grade level was identified and her performance was compared to it, for example:

Cecily, Grade 7

First-Aid Grade Level 7

First-Aid Performance Grade A

2. *Performance level appraisal:* Cecily's current grade level was identified and her work behaviors rather than skill performance were compared to it, for example:

Cecily, Grade 7

Reading grade level: 3

Reads independently: B+

Asks for assistance: B

Completes assignments independently: A

Completes homework assignments: A

3. *Individualized appraisal:* Cecily's performance is evaluated using her individualized education program (IEP) goals and objectives, for example:

Cecily, Grade 7

IEP goal: By the end of the first semester, Cecily will demonstrate competence in key first-aid skills.

Objective 1. Cecily will complete six steps in taking care of minor injuries with 100% accuracy.

✓ achieved _____ in progress

Objective 2. Cecily will complete nine steps in applying a plastic bandage with 100% accuracy.

✓ achieved _____ in progress

Objective 3. Cecily will complete 12 steps in communicating an emergency with 100% accuracy.

_____ achieved ✓ in progress

IMPROVING WORK SKILLS

It is important for students with mental retardation to gain the adaptive behavior skills they need in order to be successful in the world of work. Sometimes, work skills are addressed with functional academic interventions. Work skills include

Following directions

Being punctual

Beginning assignments promptly

Staying on task

Completing assignments

The following strategies will help you to improve the work skills of your students with mental retardation:

1. Communicate to students that attendance and punctuality are important, and "practice what you preach."

2. Keep accurate records of attendance and punctuality. Provide special activities for students with perfect or improving records.

3. Have students monitor their own attendance and punctuality. Use daily journal entries or time cards as records for this self-monitoring activity.

4. Encourage students to be punctual by scheduling special announcements. For example, announce that all students who are in their seats right now are eligible for good behavior tickets. Provide special treats (e.g., pieces of candy) for students who are on time for class.

5. Make special activities (e.g., games, videos, parties) contingent on completion of assigned tasks. Start with a small number of tasks, and gradually increase the amount of completed work necessary to earn rewards.

6. Have students record and chart the number of assignments completed each day. Review the charts periodically, and use them to make instructional planning decisions.

7. Break longer assignments into shorter units. Provide rewards and support after the completion of each smaller task.

8. Set liberal standards for task completion (e.g., one or two tasks a day). Gradually increase them after students develop appropriate work habits.

IMPROVING LEISURE SKILLS

Students with mental retardation need to learn adaptive behavior skills in order to use and enjoy their free time. Like work skills, leisure skills may be addressed in interventions. Leisure skills include

Functioning appropriately and independently during free time

Participating in recreation activities that foster social skills

Here are some ways to improve leisure skills:

1. **Identify the leisure needs of your students.** Do they understand the concept of free time? Do they have basic leisure skills (e.g., ability to play table games, interact

with others)? Do they recognize age-appropriate leisure activities? Teach skills that have not been developed.

2. **Incorporate recreation and leisure skills into existing instructional content.** For example, have students call leisure businesses to obtain information as part of a social studies unit on community resources, or use movie sections, recreation and park brochures, or other leisure activity materials.

3. **Use leisure activities to reinforce classroom instruction.** Teach students how to score a bowling game, figure win/loss records in sports, or calculate batting averages in baseball or field goal percentages in basketball. Create simple assignments for them to practice these skills.

4. **Create problem-solving situations around leisure activities, and discuss solutions to them.** If it takes 30 minutes to walk to the bowling alley, what time should you leave to be on time to meet your friends at 8:00? What alternatives do you have if you don't leave on time?

6

What Should Teachers Know About Teaching Students With Severe Disabilities?

S ome students with mental retardation (and other disabilities) need ongoing assistance to be successful in and out of school. Sometimes, these students need help getting from place to place. Sometimes, they need to use special means of communicating. The goals for these students are the same as for their neighbors and peers (e.g., independent living, employment, and self-sufficiency). Special education helps them to achieve their goals.

Andrew is in first grade. He gets around using a wheelchair. He has not developed language as his peers have, and "simple" behaviors such as feeding and dressing are extremely difficult for him.

Thirteen-year-old **Chris** has never been in a "regular" classroom or neighborhood school. School district personnel

(Continued)

(Continued)

thought Chris's behavior problems were too severe to be handled by general education teachers. Things are changing. This year Chris will attend the same middle school as the other children living in the Barclay Downs neighborhood. Teachers at the school will receive support from Chris's former special education teachers to make the transition go more smoothly. The principal of Chris's new school summarized the attitudes of everyone involved: "This will work. We want Chris to be with us, and we'll do whatever we have to do to make the time spent here successful—just like we would for any other student."

Stephanie is 23 years old. She spent most of her schooling in a special day school for students with severe retardation. Now she is living in a small group home and working at a local fast-food restaurant where she clears tables and keeps the dining area orderly and clean. A job coach from a local university program helped her find the job, learn how to use public transportation to go to work, and practice appropriate skills while working. The coach periodically checks with Stephanie and her supervisor to see how things are going.

There was a time in the not-so-distant past when students like Andrew, Chris, and Stephanie were not provided free, appropriate education, as their neighbors and peers were. There was a time when the lives of people with severe disabilities were thought to be hopeless. Today, school districts across the country are making serious efforts to develop effective ways to provide the same educational opportunities to students with severe disabilities that they provide to all other students.

DEFINITION

There is no specific category for people who require more intensive intervention or whose problems are more severe than those of others with similar disabilities or multiple disabilities. In fact, a definition for severe disabilities is not specifically included in federal guidelines for providing special education. The Association for Persons With Severe Handicaps (TASH) addresses the interests of people with severe disabilities, many of whom have traditionally been identified as having severe and profound mental retardation. TASH (Meyer, Peck, & Brown, 1991, p. 19) has provided a widely accepted definition for **severe disabilities**:

> These people include individuals of all ages who require extensive ongoing support in more than one major life activity in order to participate in integrated community settings and to enjoy a quality of life that is available to citizens with fewer or no disabilities. Support may be required for life activities such as mobility, communication, self-care, and learning as necessary for independent living, employment, and self-sufficiency.

Although any disability may be considered "severe," this term is usually reserved for a specific set of factors. People with severe disabilities generally exhibit extremely low scores on intelligence tests (i.e., more than three standard deviations below average). They also require special assistance because medical and physical problems, communication problems, or vision and hearing problems seriously limit the extent to which they will profit from ordinary life experiences.

PREVALENCE

The prevalence of severe mental retardation is difficult to determine because there is no universally accepted definition, and current federal categories and data collection procedures do not include students with severe disabilities. Estimates range from 0.1–1.0 percent of the population, and it is generally agreed that this is an important group in need of special education services. Most school districts in the country have programs for these students.

Curriculum Considerations

The curriculum for students with severe disabilities emphasizes functionality, age-appropriateness, and independence. Functional skills have applications in everyday life, including home living and community use. Learning to use public transportation and to purchase items from vending machines are examples of functional skills that are appropriate for students with severe disabilities.

All students should participate in activities that are appropriate for their age. For students with severe disabilities, this means learning functional skills and practicing them in natural environments in the presence of or interacting with peers without disabilities. Students with severe disabilities need to practice being independent, making decisions, and participating in life's experiences, just as their peers do.

Four areas of instruction are considered critical for students with severe disabilities:

Communication

Self-care

Mobility

Community living

All these skills come together to support independent community living, vocations, and recreation.

Communication

Students who can communicate verbally or in writing are more likely to have a wider range of opportunities than do their peers who are unable to speak or write. Some students with severe disabilities are able to learn to understand spoken and written language; others may not learn these skills even after extensive instruction. Alternative systems for communicating (e.g., sign language, communication boards, symbol boards, and electronic communication aids) enable these students to express their feelings in much the same way that their peers express themselves with words and written messages. Developing some form of communication is a key component of any instructional program designed to achieve functional, age-appropriate, independent behaviors.

Self-Care

The development of self-care skills begins early in the lives of students without disabilities and represents a key stage in becoming an independent, functional person. Students with severe disabilities may experience delayed development of the self-care skills that their peers without disabilities learn easily. For example, very specific instructional sequences are often used to teach eating, dressing, and toileting, as well as grooming skills such as hand washing, face washing, tooth brushing, and hair combing.

Mobility

Being able to get around in the environment also represents an important step in functionally independent, age-appropriate behavior. Movement and posture are important to independence. They are not only linked to general health and comfort, but also to participation in school and community activities. If you cannot move around easily in your environment or if you are unable to control your head, arm, or leg movements while sitting, standing, reaching and grasping, or walking, tasks are much more difficult. Mobility and movement are therefore an essential part of educational programs for students with severe disabilities. Adaptive equipment (e.g., to facilitate appropriate body positions and movements) and physical therapy (e.g., to improve flexibility, posture, and range of motion) are critical components of mobility instruction.

Community Living

Functional, age-appropriate, independent community living requires mastery of basic vocational and recreational skills.

Students with severe disabilities must be taught job-related vocational skills (such as following instructions, completing specific tasks, following rules) that their peers without disabilities often learn incidentally on the job. They require assistance finding jobs, learning and performing their jobs, and keeping jobs. They also require assistance occupying themselves constructively when they are not working. Students with severe disabilities may not learn appropriate and satisfying recreational skills without formal instruction.

INSTRUCTIONAL APPROACHES

A variety of instructional approaches are appropriate and effective in teaching communication, self-care, mobility, and community living skills to students with severe disabilities. Generally, these involve increasing appropriate behavior or decreasing inappropriate behavior to facilitate functional, age-appropriate, independent living skills. The process teachers of students with severe disabilities use is the same process other teachers use; it includes the following seven steps:

1. Assess the current level of functioning. (What can the student do relative to what is expected or desired?)

2. Define the skill to be taught. (What is the student expected to do, or what will be taught?)

3. Arrange the conditions of learning. (What sequence of steps will be used to teach the desired skill?)

4. Prompt or cue responses. (What verbal or physical messages will show the student what to do?)

5. Reinforce responses. (What feedback will be used to increase or maintain the student's behavior?)

6. Promote generalization. (What procedures will be used to ensure the behavior is exhibited in natural settings with peers and other people without disabilities?)

7. Evaluate performance. (What information will be used to judge success?)

With instructional support, students with severe disabilities can interact with their neighbors and peers and participate in community activities quite successfully. Across the U.S., students with severe mental retardation are attending classes with their nondisabled peers. In Vermont, for example, students with severe disabilities have been receiving special education supports in general education classrooms since 1984—and it's working:

> At the beginning of the year, if I was making copies of something I might forget to count Jon: I just didn't deal with him. . . . When I count the kids in my class now, I've counted Jon. It just took me a while. (Giangreco, Dennis, Cloninger, Edelman, & Schattman, 1993, p. 359)

To better serve students with disabilities, school districts have adopted five principles when placing students in neighborhood programs:

1. Place students with disabilities in schools as close as possible to those attended by neighbors and peers.

2. Place them in age-appropriate schools.

3. Place them in schools and classrooms where principals and other personnel support **inclusion** (providing educational experiences with natural neighbors and peers to the maximum extent possible).

4. Avoid placing them in schools with large numbers of students with other disabilities.

5. Avoid having their classes in isolated, nonacademic areas of the school.

7

What Trends and Issues Influence How We Teach Students With Mental Retardation?

Deciding where and how students with disabilities should receive education is not easy, and it will continue to be an important issue in special education, especially as it relates to mental retardation. Concepts like **normalization** (treating people with disabilities like everybody else) and the **least restrictive environment** (educating students with disabilities in general education programs as much as possible) constitute the provisions of federal legislation, and they direct that the lives of students with mental retardation should be as "normal" as possible. But, compared to other students with disabilities, students with mental retardation are more likely to receive educational services in more restrictive placements (U.S. Department of Education, 2002). Some professionals believe that separate classrooms and special school programs represent the best placements for students with mental retardation. They claim that these settings provide the best opportunities for delivering the special instruction necessary for success. Others argue that separation from normal society is not positive. They promote full participation and integration of students with mental retardation in the same experiences as their neighbors and peers. There's no simple answer to the question of where special education should be provided, and concerns related to treatment are continuously debated.

PREVENTION OF MENTAL RETARDATION

Many causes of mental retardation are preventable; many professionals believe that more than half of all cases of mental retardation could have been prevented (Ysseldyke & Algozzine, 1990). There has been a continuing concern for prevention and early intervention. As illustrated in *Table 7.1*, many of the strategies for controlling mental retardation are simple. The issue is more one of why (e.g., Why has society been so slow in implementing prevention strategies?) rather than one of what should be done to prevent mental retardation.

Table 7.1   Top Ten Ways to Prevent Mental Retardation

1. Obtain proper medical care, and maintain good maternal health and nutrition during pregnancy.

2. Prevent and treat infections during pregnancy.

3. Help parents avoid sexually transmitted diseases.

4. Encourage parents to plan and space pregnancies and to seek genetic counseling and proper prenatal tests.

5. Ensure proper nutrition, immunization, and general medical care for all children.

6. Keep homes, vehicles, schools, and communities safe.

7. Create appropriate educational programs.

8. Educate parents, and provide support in parenting skills.

9. Protect children from abuse and neglect.

10. Provide public education on the causes of mental retardation

Transitioning From School to Work

In addition to preventing and controlling retardation in young children before they enter school, professionals are concerned in the treatment of people with retardation who have left school programs. Not too long ago, many adults with mental retardation were segregated in institutions. Today, more and more people with retardation are living in natural environments. A need for people and services concerned with successful transition has arisen.

Individualized Transition Plans

Many students with mental retardation make the transition from school to job placements and work under the supervision of special education personnel. An **individual transition plan (ITP)** is part of the student's IEP. While the IEP focuses on educational goals and objectives to be achieved during the school year, the ITP addresses skills (e.g., making leisure choices, being able to shop, job placement assistance) and supportive services (e.g., vocational rehabilitation) required outside of school and in the future. The ITP attempts to coordinate assistance provided by outside agencies and the school. A typical ITP delimits instruction to be completed in the community and lists referral agencies for job placement and on-the-job services.

Graduation

In recent years, students with mental retardation were among the least likely to graduate from high school (U.S. Department of Education, 2002); and, compared to students with learning disabilities or communication disorders, more students with mental retardation graduated through the certificate method (i.e., receiving nontraditional diplomas). The percentage of students with mental retardation who dropped out (about 22 percent) was slightly below that for all other students receiving special education (U.S. Department of Education, 1993).

Follow-up studies have indicated that the majority of special education graduates do not make a successful transition from school to life as adults in their local communities. Many remain underemployed or unemployed despite participating in successful "transition" experiences.

Self-Determination

Some professionals argue that students' lack of success after graduation is due to a lack of decision-making skills and the unnatural experiences fostered by special education. This concern has spawned an interest in supporting full participation of people with disabilities in natural settings in the community and greater emphasis on teaching them to make choices. **Self-determination** (the ability to consider options and make appropriate choices at home, during school, at work, and during leisure time) has become the battle cry of professionals, parents, and people with disabilities—and probably will continue to be so.

8

Mental Retardation in Perspective

M ental retardation is one of the oldest special education categories. Providing assistance to people with mental retardation and severe disabilities has come a long way. In early Greek society, a council of elders examined infants. If the children were weak or disabled, they were left to die in the mountains. In early Roman society, children who were blind, deaf, or mentally dull were thrown by their parents into the Tiber River. Throughout early European and Asian history, people who were thought to be retarded were excluded from society. Things are very different today.

RECENT ADVANCES

Changes in the treatment of people with mental retardation came from the work of professionals who demonstrated that those with mental retardation could be helped and who argued for their humane treatment. In 1972, the Pennsylvania Association for Retarded Citizens (PARC) sued the Pennsylvania Department of Education, claiming denial of services to children with mental retardation. Based on the decision in *Pennsylvania*

Association of Retarded Citizens v. Commonwealth of Pennsylvania (1972), the state's school districts were forced to locate, assess, and plan an appropriate educational program for students with mental retardation who had been excluded from school. This legal decision was one of the primary forces behind the enactment of the Education for All Handicapped Children Act of 1975 (Public Law 94-142).

Through litigation—as well as through the activity of advocacy groups, such as the Association for Retarded Citizens (ARC), the Council for Exceptional Children (CEC), and the American Association on Mental Retardation (AAMR), and because of the efforts of powerful people, such as the Kennedys and Hubert Humphrey—treatment and services for students with mental retardation and severe disabilities have improved dramatically.

Today many people with mental retardation are taking control of their own lives. This movement, known as self-advocacy or self-determination, is one more example of the desire of people with mental retardation to be treated just like everybody else.

Window on Practice

Cecelia, a 15-year-old freshman with Down's syndrome, had never taken a program of general education classes before September of 1992. When her parents proposed enrolling her in her neighborhood high school, school officials resisted. They noted that the school had no special education program for students with severe disabilities. After Cecelia did multiplication, division, word problems, and fractions for the first time, her father was asked why she hadn't done this type of work before. He replied, "Because no one challenged her to do it, that's why."

There was a time when people with Down's syndrome, like Cecelia, or with other types of mental retardation or severe disabilities would simply not be educated. Today, "we've come a long way," but obstacles remain. In the future, people with mental retardation and severe disabilities will be educated and treated just like their neighbors and peers are.

A person who is severely impaired never knows his hidden
sources of strength until he is treated like a normal human
being and encouraged to shape his own life.

—Helen Keller

THE IMPORTANCE OF ENVIRONMENTS

Students with mental retardation require extra assistance to
learn what their peers learn without special assistance. The goal
of this assistance should be to foster independence within environments that are, as much as possible, like those experienced by
neighbors and peers.

The environments in which students with severe intellectual
disabilities receive instructional services have critical effects on
where and how they spend their postschool lives. Segregation
begets segregation.

When students attend segregated schools, they are denied
opportunities to function in integrated environments and activities. Their peers without disabilities do not know or understand
them and too often think negatively of them; their parents
become afraid to risk allowing them opportunities to learn to
function in integrated environments later in life; and taxpayers
assume that they need to be sequestered in segregated group
homes, enclaves, work crews, activity centers, sheltered work-
shops, institutions, and nursing homes (Brown et al., 1989).

INCLUSION

Continuing efforts to include all people with disabilities in all
aspects of life are essential. Neighborhood schools should serve
all students in the neighborhood. They should be inclusive places,
where activities and learning experiences are available to all
students and a wide range of services are provided. Schools
need to take responsibility for educating students with mental
retardation and other students with disabilities. Responsibility

for bringing services to these students rests with the entire professional staff, not just with special education personnel. Although significant progress has been made in making schools inclusive, there is still plenty of room for improvement. As an educator, you can help make the difference.

9

What Have We Learned?

As you complete your study of teaching students with mental retardation, it may be helpful to review what you have learned. To help you check your understanding, we have listed the key points and key vocabulary for you to review. We have included the Self-Assessment again, so you can compare what you know now with what you knew as you began your study. Finally, we provide a few topics for you to think about and some activities for you to do "on your own."

KEY POINTS

◉ Mental retardation is one of the oldest categories in special education.

◉ The term refers to people who have both difficulty learning and consistent delays in adaptive behavior and development.

◉ Professionals use scores on intelligence tests and measures of adaptive behavior as indications of learning and development.

◙ Academic instruction is the most common area in which teachers must accommodate students with mild mental retardation.

◙ The goal of education for students with mental retardation focuses on preparing them for adult life by teaching functional academic skills, school adaptive behavior skills, and leisure and work skills.

◙ Instruction for students with mental retardation is more focused on everyday life experiences than it is for their peers.

◙ Students with severe disabilities exhibit extremely low scores on intelligence tests and require special assistance because medical and physical problems, communication problems, or vision and hearing problems seriously limit the extent to which they will profit from ordinary life experiences.

◙ Students with severe disabilities require assistance with communication, self-care, mobility, and community living skills to be successful in everyday life.

◙ Employment is the single most important concern for those who work with adults with mental retardation and severe disabilities.

◙ History is full of incidents of less than favorable treatment of people with mental retardation and severe disabilities, but treatment is improving as a result of legal action and concern for normalization and inclusion.

KEY VOCABULARY

Adaptive behavior, sometimes called adaptive functioning, is a person's ability to learn and apply life skills in ways that enable him or her to live independently.

Adaptive behavior scales typically contain items related to self-care, communication, academic and social skills, home living, community use, health, safety, and work.

Down's syndrome is a condition in which the twenty first set of chromosomes is a triplet rather than a pair.

Individual transition plan (ITP) is part of a student's IEP and addresses the skills (e.g., making leisure choices, being able to shop, job placement assistance) and supportive services (e.g., vocational rehabilitation) required outside of school and in the future.

Individualized education program (IEP) is a specially designed plan that documents current levels of performance; the goals, objectives, and services for improving that performance; and the dates on which services will be provided, who will provide them, and how they will be monitored to ensure success.

Individualized family services plan describes the unique family needs of an individual with mental retardation and the services that will address those needs.

Intellectual functioning is the person's ability to learn, think, solve problems, and make sense of the world.

Klinefelter's syndrome is a combination of physical abnormalities that typically results from aberrations in the sex chromosomes—pair 23 (the male has an extra X chromosome).

Least restrictive environment means educating students with disabilities in general education programs as much as possible.

Mental retardation is a disability characterized by significant limitations both in intellectual functioning and in adaptive behavior as expressed in conceptual, social, and practical adaptive skills.

Noncategorical means not formally labeling individuals to provide services to them.

Normalization means treating people with disabilities like everybody else.

Phenylketonuria (PKU) is an inherited genetic metabolic disorder in which the enzyme required to digest phenylalanine (PHE), a part of protein, is missing.

Self-determination is the ability to consider options and make appropriate choices at home, during school, at work, and during leisure time.

Task analysis means breaking complex skills into component parts to establish an appropriate teaching sequence and to decide which skill to teach first (least complex).

Self-Assessment 2

Afteryou complete this book, check your knowledge and understanding of the content covered. Choose the best answer for each of the following questions.

1. Individuals with mental retardation

   a. do not need to master academic skills

   b. need special assistance to learn what many of their peers learn incidentally

   c. do not have the intelligence to read or do mathematics

   d. represent the largest group of individuals with disabilities receiving special education

2. Even though many states use a variety of terminology to label students who have below average intelligence scores, most of the students

   a. will not be able to live independently

   b. will probably not be able to get a job

   c. have average to low intelligence with average adaptive functioning levels

   d. have significantly subaverage intellectual and adaptive functioning skills

3. There are reasons other than mental retardation that might cause a person to achieve a below average score on an intelligence test, including

   a. civic differences

   b. economic differences

    c. climate differences

    d. cultural differences

4. The addition of _____ to the definition of mental retardation began to improve the problem of overrepresentation of minority students in special education classes.

    a. the adaptive behavior qualifier

    b. the intelligence quotient

    c. current level of functioning

    d. variation in student behavior

5. The definition of mental retardation states that the disability must be diagnosed before the age of

    a. 3

    b. 5

    c. 18

    d. 21

6. According to the definition of mental retardation, how many adaptive skill areas must be limited?

    a. one

    b. more than one

    c. two

    d. more than two

7. Students diagnosed with mental retardation must have an intelligence test score of _____ or below on one or more individually administered general intelligence tests.

    a. 50–55

    b. 60–65

c. 70–75

d. 80–85.

8. A student fits the definition of mental retardation if

a. social problems are prominent

b. adaptive functioning skills are adequate

c. adaptive functioning skills are intact

d. measured intelligence is significantly subaverage

9. The effectiveness with which an individual meets the standards of personal independence and social responsibility expected of his or her age and cultural group is defined as

a. adaptive behavior

b. social behavior

c. peer tolerance behavior

d. responsible, age-appropriate behavior

10. Adaptive behavior scales may include all of the following except

a. self-care skills

b. academic skills

c. social skills

d. home living skills

REFLECTION

After you answer the multiple-choice questions, think about how you would answer the following questions:

- What factors might affect the academic success of individuals with mental retardation?
- What are some causes for mental retardation?
- What do effective teachers do to provide support for students with mental retardation?

Answer Key for Self-Assessments

1. b

2. d

3. d

4. a

5. c

6. b

7. c

8. d

9. a

10. b

On Your Own

☑ Imagine that you are a teacher who has several students with mental retardation in your classroom. What decisions would you have to make to help these students be successful? What instructional approaches would be appropriate for working with them? What specific activities would you use to adapt a lesson you were teaching to your class on measurement?

☑ Attend a parents' group that is concerned with the education of students with mental retardation. List the topics that are discussed. Interview at least three parents to obtain their overall impressions of the services being provided by the school system to their children.

☑ Check your local newspaper for evidence of bias, prejudice, or stereotypical thinking about people with mental retardation. Find articles and news stories that portray people with mental retardation favorably, and write a letter to the editor supporting the work the newspaper did. If you find a negative portrayal, write a letter educating the paper as to a better way to present information about people with mental retardation.

☑ Contact a local, state, or national organization that focuses on people with mental retardation. Identify the purpose of the organization, its membership, and its services.

☑ Look in the Yellow Pages of your local phone book for agencies that serve people with mental retardation. Call several, and ask about the kinds of services they provide and how they work with school personnel to meet the needs of these students and their families.

Resources

BOOKS

American Association on Mental Retardation. (2002). *Mental retardation: Definition, classification, and systems of supports* (10th ed.). Annapolis, MD: Author. This latest edition of this classic resource presents a complete system to define and diagnose mental retardation, to classify and describe strengths and limitations, and to plan a support, needs profile.

Beirne-Smith, M., Ittenbach, R. F., & Patton, J. R. (2002). *Mental retardation* (6th ed.). Upper Saddle River, NJ: Prentice Hall. This is an introductory textbook describing causes, assessment, and teaching approaches.

Bergman, T. (1989). *We laugh, we love, we cry: Children living with mental retardation*. Milwaukee, WI: Gareth Stevens. This story about two sisters experiencing mental retardation is excellent for elementary school students.

Byars, B. (1970). *The summer of the swans*. New York: Viking. This is the story of Sara, a 14-year-old with all the joys of adolescence, and of how her life changes when her brother with mental retardation disappears.

Cipani, E., & Spooner, F. (1994). *Curricular and instructional approaches for persons with severe disabilities*. Needham Heights, MA: Allyn & Bacon. This edited text addresses key areas of instruction for people with severe disabilities, including principles underlying behavior change, curricular domain, and key service delivery issues and approaches.

Drew, C. J., & Hardman, M. L. (2000). *Mental retardation: A life cycle approach* (7th ed.). Upper Saddle River, NJ: Prentice Hall. This comprehensive introduction to mental retardation, based on the stages of human development, provides an interdisciplinary perspective on diagnosis and intervention—from conception through adulthood.

Dykens, E. M., Hodapp, R. M., & Finucane, B. M. (2000). *Genetics and mental retardation syndromes: A new look at behavior and interventions.* Baltimore, MD: Paul H. Brookes. The genetic causes of mental retardation are being discovered, and every day more people are diagnosed with specific syndromes. This comprehensive guide identifies characteristics of syndromes, so you'll be able to provide better interventions and create wider community inclusion.

Edwards, J., & Dawson, D. (1983). *My friend David: A source book about Down syndrome and a personal story about friendship.* New York: Ednick Communications. The first part of this book is a handwritten autobiography written by David Dawson, a man with mental retardation.

Garrigue, S. (1978). *Between friends.* New York: Scholastic. In this book for upper elementary and middle school students, Jill learns about retardation through her friendship with Dedi.

Kaufman, S. Z. (1999). *Retarded isn't stupid, mom!* (Rev. ed.). Baltimore, MD: Paul H. Brookes. What is it like to grow up with mental retardation? How do parents and families cope with the challenges and frustrations of daily life? Sandra Kaufman, with her daughter's assistance, describes the joys and sorrows of raising a child with mental retardation.

MacMillan, D. L. (1982). *Mental retardation in school and society* (2nd ed.). Boston: Little, Brown. This is an introductory textbook describing definitions, levels of retardation, causes, and interventions.

Meyer, L. H., Peck, C. A., & Brown, L. (1991). *Critical issues in the lives of people with severe disabilities*. Baltimore, MD: Paul H. Brookes. Considered by many to be the primary book for those interested in people with severe disabilities, this text explores the six major resolutions passed by The Association for Persons With Severe Handicaps. Definitions and diagnosis, deinstitutionalization and community services, redefinition of a continuum of services, extensions of law and educational services, adult services, and life and death issues are addressed.

Nobel, V. (1993). *Down is up for Aaron Eagle*. San Francisco, CA: Harper. This is a mother's story of living and growing with a child with Down's syndrome.

Polloway, E. A., Patton, J. R., & Serna, L. (2001). *Strategies for teaching learners with special needs* (7th ed.). Upper Saddle River, NJ: Prentice Hall. This is an introductory textbook describing teaching methods.

Robinson, N. M., & Robinson, H. B. (1976). *The mentally retarded child: A psychological approach* (2nd ed.). New York: McGraw-Hill. Considered a classic, this introductory textbook describes the definitions and causes of mental retardation and presents information on levels of retardation and interventions.

Shyer, M. F. (1978). *Welcome home, jellybean*. New York: Macmillan. Upper elementary and middle school students will enjoy this story about a twelve-year-old boy who encounters major difficulties when his older sister with mental retardation comes home to stay.

Snell, M. E. (1993). *Instruction of students with severe disabilities* (4th ed.). New York: Macmillan. This edited text addresses key areas of instruction for people with severe disabilities, including assessment and functional skill intervention in key curriculum areas.

Trainer, M. (1991). *Differences in common: Straight talk on mental retardation, Down syndrome, and life.* Bethesda, MD: Woodbine House. Telephone: (800) 843-7323.

Wehmeyer, M. L. (2002). *Teaching students with mental retardation. Providing access to the general curriculum.* Baltimore, MD: Paul H. Brookes. Every day, teachers and education professionals struggle with a crucial classroom goal: ensuring that students with mental retardation have access to the general curriculum. This book provides guidance, research, and practical strategies for achieving this goal.

Westling, D. (1986). *Introduction to mental retardation.* Englewood Cliffs, NJ: Prentice Hall. This introductory textbook describes definitions, levels of retardation, causes, and interventions.

JOURNALS AND ARTICLES

American Journal on Mental Retardation (AJMR). Published by the American Association on Mental Retardation, this scientific and archival multidisciplinary journal focuses on mental retardation, its causes, treatment, and prevention. It includes original research on characteristics, individual differences, and factors that alter characteristics; theoretical interpretations of research; and reports of evaluative research on new treatment approaches. Dr. Stephen R. Schroeder, 1052 Dole Human Development Center, University of Kansas, Lawrence, KS 66045.

Education and Training in Mental Retardation (ETMR). This publication of the Council for Exceptional Children (Mental Retardation and Developmental Disabilities Division) focuses on the education and welfare of persons who are retarded. It includes research, expository manuscripts, and critical reviews of the literature, especially on identification and assessment, educational programming, characteristics, training of instructional personnel, habilitation, prevention, community understanding and provisions, and legislation.

Dr. Stanley H. Zucker, Editor, Special Education Program, Farmer 305, Arizona State University, Tempe, AZ 85287–2001.

Journal of Intellectual Disability Research (JIDR). *JIDR* is devoted exclusively to the scientific study of mental deficiency. It includes clinical case reports; pathological reports; biochemical investigations; articles on genetics and cytogenetics; psychological, educational, and sociological studies; and the results of animal experiments. Editor, *Journal of Intellectual Disability Research,* University of Wales, College of Medicine, 55 Park Place, Cardiff CF1 3AT, South Glamorgan, Wales, United Kingdom.

Journal of the Association for Persons With Severe Handicaps (JASH). *JASH* reports original research and reviews literature that addresses service delivery, program development, assessment, and intervention for people with severe disabilities. *JASH* is published quarterly by The Association for Persons With Severe Handicaps (TASH). TASH, 11202 Greenwood Avenue North, Seattle, WA 98133 or Jim Halle, Editor, *JASH*, Department of Special Education, University of Illinois, Champaign, IL 61820.

Mental Retardation (MR). Published by the American Association on Mental Retardation, *MR* is a journal of policy, practices, and perspectives in the field of mental retardation. As a publication with an applied focus, it publishes essays, qualitative and quantitative research articles, conceptual papers, comprehensive reviews, case studies, policy analyses, and innovative practice descriptions and evaluations. Dr. Steven J. Taylor, Editor, *MR*, Center on Human Policy, 200 Huntington Hall, Syracuse, NY 13244–2340.

Research in Developmental Disabilities (RDD) publishes original research, reviews of literature, and conceptual papers that address theory and behavioral research related to people with severe and pervasive developmental disabilities. Editor, *RDD*, Pergamon Press, Maxwell House, Fairview Park, Elmsford, NY 10523.

ORGANIZATIONS

American Association on Mental Retardation (AAMR)

Established in 1876, AAMR is comprised of physicians, educators, administrators, social workers, psychologists, psychiatrists, and others interested in the general welfare of persons with mental retardation and in studying the causes, treatments, and prevention of mental retardation. AAMR facilitates research and provides information for professional development. AAMR, 444 North Capitol Street NW, Suite 846, Washington, DC 20001. (202) 387-1968; (800) 424-3688. *www.aamr.org*.

Division on Career Development (DCD)

Founded in 1976, DCD includes members of the Council for Exceptional Children who teach or in other ways work toward the career development and vocational education of people with disabilities. DCD promotes research, legislation, information dissemination, and technical assistance. DCD, Council for Exceptional Children, 1100 North Glebe Road, Suite 300, Arlington, VA 22201–5704.

Division on Mental Retardation and Developmental Disabilities

Founded in 1964, the Council for Exceptional Children's Division on Mental Retardation and Developmental Disabilities (CEC-MRDD) advances professional growth and research to promote programs for individuals with mental retardation and developmental disabilities. With 6,800 members, including teachers, teacher educators, administrators, researchers, and other professionals, it is one of the largest CEC divisions. CEC-MRDD members receive professional journals and have access to resources. CEC-MRDD, Council for Exceptional Children, 1100 North Glebe Road, Suite 300, Arlington, VA 22201–5704. (888) 232-7733; (703) 620-3660; (703) 264-9446 *TTY*. cec@cec.sped.org. *www.mrddcec.org*.

National Information Center for Children and Youth With Disabilities (NICHCY)

NICHCY provides information and education on disability-related issues. P.O. Box 1492, Washington, DC 20013. (800) 695-0285 (Voice/TTY). nichcy@aed.org. *www.nichcy.org.*

The Association for Persons With Severe Handicaps (TASH)

TASH is dedicated to people perceived as having severe intellectual disabilities and seeks to build an inclusive society that values all people. TASH membership consists of people with disabilities, families, professionals, and community members. TASH is committed to creating communities where no one is segregated and everyone belongs; forming new alliances that embrace diversity; eradicating injustices and inequities; research, education, legislation and litigation; and excellence in services. TASH, 11202 Greenwood Avenue North, Seattle, WA 98133.

The Association for Retarded Citizens (ARC)

ARC was founded in 1950 as an organization for parents, professionals, and others interested in mental retardation. Its work at local, state, and national levels promotes appropriate treatment, research, public understanding, and legislation for people with mental retardation. ARC, 1010 Wayne Avenue, Suite 650, Silver Spring, MD 20910. (301) 565-3842. info@thearc.org. *www.thearc.org.* For publications: *www.thearcpub.com.*

References

American Association on Mental Retardation. (1992). *Mental retardation: Definition, classification, and systems of support—Workbook.* Washington, DC: Author.

American Association on Mental Retardation. (2002a). *Definition of Mental Retardation.* Retrieved January 1, 2006, from http://www.aamr.org/Policies/faq_mental_retardation.shtml.

American Association on Mental Retardation. (2002b). *Mental retardation definition, classification, and systems of supports* (10th ed.). Washington, DC: Author.

Brown, L., Long, E., Udvari-Solner, A., Davis, L., VanDeventer, P., Ahlgren, C., Johnson, F., Gruenewald, L., & Jorgensen, J. (1989). The home school: Why students with severe intellectual disabilities must attend the schools of their brothers, sisters, friends, and neighbors. *Journal of the Association for Persons With Severe Handicaps, 14,* 1–7.

Education for All Handicapped Children Act, Pub. L. No. 94-142, 89 Stat. 773 (1975).

Giangreco, M. F., Dennis, R., Cloninger, C., Edelman, S., & Schattman, R. (1993). "I've counted Jon": Transformational experiences of teachers educating students with disabilities. *Exceptional Children, 59,* 359–372.

Grossman, H. (Ed.). (1983). *Manual on terminology and classification in mental retardation* (Rev. ed.). Washington, DC: American Association on Mental Deficiency.

Individuals With Disabilities Education Act, 34 U.S.C. § 300.7 (1990).

Individuals With Disabilities Education Act: Federal Regulations, 34 C.F.R. § 300.7 (1997).

Meyer, L. H., Peck, C. A., & Brown, L. (1991). *Critical issues in the lives of people with severe disabilities.* Baltimore, MD: Paul H. Brookes.

Pennsylvania Association of Retarded Citizens v. Commonwealth of Pennsylvania, 343 F. Supp. 279 (E.D. Pa. 1972).

Spooner, F., Stem, B., & Test, D. W. (1989). Teaching first aid skills to students who are moderately mentally handicapped. *Education and Training in Mental Retardation, 24,* 341–351.

Stem, B., & Test, D. W. (1989). Teaching first aid skills in the classroom. *Teaching Exceptional Children*, 22(1), 10–12.

U.S. Department of Education. (2002). *Twenty-fourth annual report to Congress on the implementation of the Individuals With Disabilities Education Act*. Washington, DC: Author.

Ysseldyke, J. E., & Algozzine, B. (1990). *Introduction to special education*. Boston: Houghton Mifflin.

Index

**CORWIN
PRESS**

The Corwin Press logo—a raven striding across an open book—represents the union of courage and learning. Corwin Press is committed to improving education for all learners by publishing books and other professional development resources for those serving the field of PreK–12 education. By providing practical, hands-on materials, Corwin Press continues to carry out the promise of its motto: **"Helping Educators Do Their Work Better."**